CW00539336

Francis Frith's
Around Southend

Photographic Memories

Francis Frith's
Around Southend

Frances Clamp

First published in the United Kingdom in 2001 by
Frith Book Company Ltd

Paperback Edition 2001
ISBN 1-85937-313-5

Hardback Edition 2001
ISBN 1-85937-408-5

British Library Cataloguing in Publication Data

Francis Frith's Around Southend
Frances Clamp

Frith Book Company Ltd
Frith's Barn, Teffont,
Salisbury, Wiltshire SP3 5QP
Tel: +44 (0) 1722 716 376
Email: info@francisfrith.co.uk
www.francisfrith.co.uk

Printed and bound in Great Britain

AS WITH ANY HISTORICAL DATABASE THE FRITH ARCHIVE IS CONSTANTLY BEING CORRECTED AND IMPROVED
AND THE PUBLISHERS WOULD WELCOME INFORMATION ON OMISSIONS OR INACCURACIES

Contents

Francis Frith: *Victorian Pioneer*

FRANCIS FRITH, Victorian founder of the world-famous photographic archive, was a complex and multi-talented man. A devout Quaker and a highly successful Victorian businessman, he was both philosophic by nature and pioneering in outlook.

By 1855 Francis Frith had already established a wholesale grocery business in Liverpool, and sold it for the astonishing sum of £200,000, which is the equivalent today of over £15,000,000. Now a multi-millionaire, he was able to indulge his passion for travel. As a child he had pored over travel books written by early explorers, and his fancy and imagination had been stirred by family holidays to the sublime mountain regions of Wales and Scotland. 'What a land of spirit-stirring and enriching scenes and places!' he had written. He was to return to these scenes of grandeur in later years to 'recapture the thousands of vivid and tender memories', but with a different purpose. Now in his thirties, and captivated by the new science of photography, Frith set out on a series of pioneering journeys to the Nile regions that occupied him from 1856 until 1860.

Intrigue and Adventure

He took with him on his travels a specially-designed wicker carriage that acted as both dark-room and sleeping chamber. These far-flung journeys were packed with intrigue and adventure. In his life story, written when he was sixty-three, Frith tells of being held captive by bandits, and of fighting 'an awful midnight battle to the very point of surrender with a deadly pack of hungry, wild dogs'. Sporting flowing Arab costume, Frith arrived at Akaba by camel seventy years before Lawrence, where he encountered 'desert princes and rival sheikhs, blazing with jewel-hilted swords'.

During these extraordinary adventures he was assiduously exploring the desert regions bordering the Nile and patiently recording the antiquities and peoples with his camera. He was the first photographer to venture beyond the sixth cataract. Africa was still the mysterious 'Dark Continent', and Stanley and Livingstone's historic meeting was a decade into the future. The conditions for picture taking confound belief. He laboured for hours in his wicker dark-room in the sweltering heat of the desert, while the volatile chemicals fizzed dangerously in their trays. Often he was forced to work in remote tombs and caves where conditions were cooler. Back in London he exhibited his photographs and was 'rapturously cheered' by members of the Royal Society. His reputation as a photographer was made overnight. An eminent modern historian has likened their impact on the population of the time to that on our own generation of the first photographs taken on the surface of the moon.

Venture of a Life-Time

Characteristically, Frith quickly spotted the opportunity to create a new business as a specialist publisher of photographs. He lived in an era of immense and sometimes violent change. For the poor in the early part of Victoria's reign work was a drudge and the hours long, and people had precious little free time to enjoy themselves. Most had no transport other than a cart or gig at their disposal, and had not travelled far beyond the boundaries of their own town or village. However, by the 1870s, the railways had threaded their way across the country, and Bank Holidays and half-day Saturdays had been made obligatory by Act of Parliament. All of a sudden the ordinary working man and his family were able to enjoy days out and see a little more of the world.

With characteristic business acumen, Francis Frith foresaw that these new tourists would enjoy having souvenirs to commemorate their days out. In 1860 he married Mary Ann Rosling and set out with the intention of photographing every city, town and village in Britain. For the next thirty years he travelled the country by train and by pony and trap, producing fine photographs of seaside resorts and beauty spots that were keenly bought by millions of Victorians. These prints were painstakingly pasted into family albums and pored over during the dark nights of winter, rekindling precious memories of summer excursions.

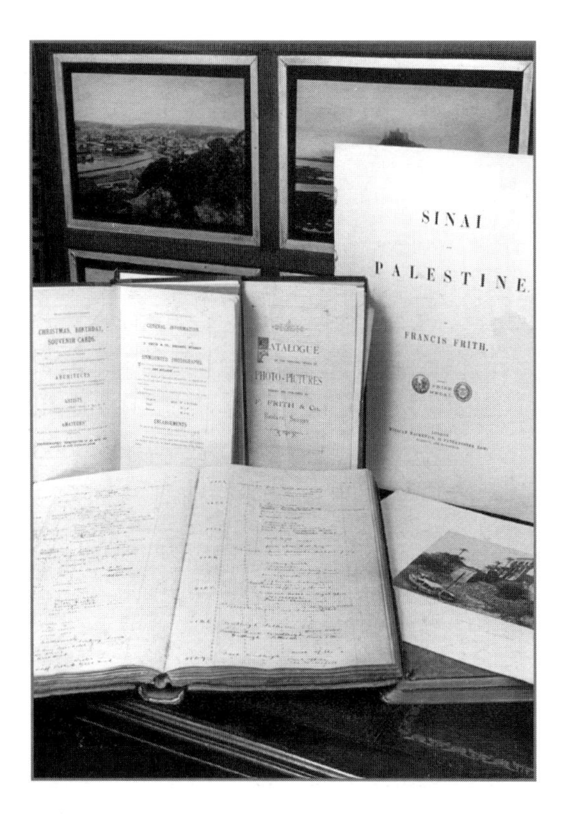

The Rise of Frith & Co

Frith's studio was soon supplying retail shops all over the country. To meet the demand he gathered about him a small team of photographers, and published the work of independent artist-photographers of the calibre of Roger Fenton and Francis Bedford. In order to gain some understanding of the scale of Frith's business one only has to look at the catalogue issued by Frith & Co in 1886: it runs to some 670 pages, listing not only many thousands of views of the British Isles but also many photographs of most European countries, and China, Japan, the USA and Canada – note the sample page shown above from the hand-written *Frith & Co* ledgers detailing pictures taken. By 1890 Frith had created the greatest specialist photographic publishing company in the world,

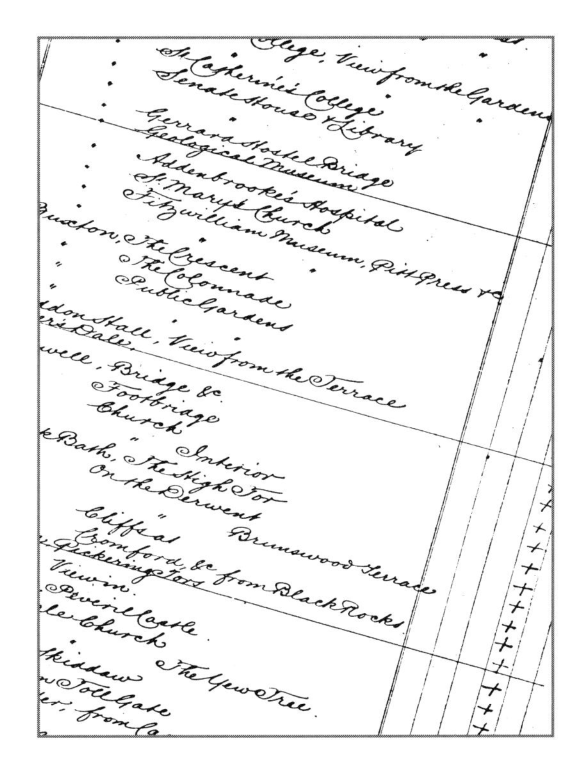

...llege, View from the Gardens
St Catherine's College
Senate House & Library
Gerrard Hostel Bridge
Geological Museum
Addenbrooke's Hospital
St Mary's Church
Fitzwilliam Museum, Pitt Press &c
Buxton, The Crescent
The Colonnade
Public Gardens
...don Hall, View from the Terrace
...'s Dale
...well, Bridge &c.
Footbridge
Church
...Bath, Interior
The High Tor
On the Derwent
Cliffs at
Brunswood Terrace
Cromford, &c from Black Rocks
Pickering Tors
View in
Peveril Castle
...le Church
The Yew Tree
Skiddaw
...Toll Gate
...er, from Ca...

with over 2,000 outlets – more than the combined number that Boots and WH Smith have today! The picture on the right shows the *Frith & Co* display board at Ingleton in the Yorkshire Dales. Beautifully constructed with mahogany frame and gilt inserts, it could display up to a dozen local scenes.

Postcard Bonanza

The ever-popular holiday postcard we know today took many years to develop. In 1870 the Post Office issued the first plain cards, with a pre-printed stamp on one face. In 1894 they allowed other publishers' cards to be sent through the mail with an attached adhesive halfpenny stamp. Demand grew rapidly, and in 1895 a new size of postcard was permitted called the court card, but there was little room for illustration. In 1899, a year after Frith's death, a new card measuring 5.5 x 3.5 inches became the standard format, but it was not until 1902 that the divided back came into being, with address and message on one face and a full-size illustration on the other. *Frith & Co* were in the vanguard of postcard development, and Frith's sons Eustace and Cyril continued their father's monumental task, expanding the number of views offered to the public and recording more and more places in Britain, as the coasts and countryside were opened up to mass travel.

Francis Frith died in 1898 at his villa in Cannes, his great project still growing. The archive he created continued in business for another seventy years. By 1970 it contained over a third of a million pictures of 7,000 cities, towns and villages. The massive photographic record Frith has left to us stands as a living monument to a special and very remarkable man.

Frith's Archive: *A Unique Legacy*

Francis Frith's legacy to us today is of immense significance and value, for the magnificent archive of evocative photographs he created provides a unique record of change in 7,000 cities, towns and villages throughout Britain over a century and more. Frith and his fellow studio photographers revisited locations many times down the years to update their views, compiling for us an enthralling and colourful pageant of British life and character.

We tend to think of Frith's sepia views of Britain as nostalgic, for most of us use them to conjure up memories of places in our own lives with which we have family associations. It often makes us forget that to Francis Frith they were records of daily life as it was actually being lived in the cities, towns and villages of his day. The Victorian age was one of great and often bewildering change for ordinary people, and though the pictures evoke an impression of slower times, life was as busy and hectic as it is today.

We are fortunate that Frith was a photographer of the people, dedicated to recording the minutiae of everyday life. For it is this sheer wealth of visual data, the painstaking chronicle of changes in dress, transport, street layouts, buildings, housing, engineering and landscape that captivates us so much today. His remarkable images offer us a powerful link with the past and with the lives of our ancestors.

See Frith at www.francisfrith.co.uk

Today's Technology

Computers have now made it possible for Frith's many thousands of images to be accessed almost instantly. In the Frith archive today, each photograph is carefully 'digitised' then stored on a CD Rom. Frith archivists can locate a single photograph amongst thousands within seconds. Views can be catalogued and sorted under a variety of categories of place and content to the immediate benefit of researchers.

Inexpensive reference prints can be created for them at the touch of a mouse button, and a wide range of books and other printed materials assembled and published for a wider, more general readership - in the next twelve months over a hundred Frith local history titles will be published! The day-to-day workings of the archive are very different from how they were in Francis Frith's time: imagine the herculean task of sorting through eleven tons of glass negatives as Frith had to do to locate a particular sequence of pictures! Yet the archive still prides itself on maintaining the same high standards of excellence laid down by Francis Frith, including the painstaking cataloguing and indexing of every view.

It is curious to reflect on how the internet now allows researchers in America and elsewhere greater instant access to the archive than Frith himself ever enjoyed. Many thousands of individual views can be called up on screen within seconds on one of the Frith internet sites, enabling people living continents away to revisit the streets of their ancestral home town, or view places in Britain where they have enjoyed holidays. Many overseas researchers welcome the chance to view special theme selections, such as transport, sports, costume and ancient monuments.

We are certain that Francis Frith would have heartily approved of these modern developments in imaging techniques, for he himself was always working at the very limits of Victorian photographic technology.

The Value of the Archive Today

Because of the benefits brought by the computer, Frith's images are increasingly studied by social historians, by researchers into genealogy and ancestory, by architects, town planners, and by teachers and schoolchildren involved in local history projects.

In addition, the archive offers every one of us an opportunity to examine the places where we and our families have lived and worked down the years. Highly successful in Frith's own era, the archive is now, a century and more on, entering a new phase of popularity.

The Past in Tune with the Future

Historians consider the Francis Frith Collection to be of prime national importance. It is the only archive of its kind remaining in private ownership and has been valued at a million pounds. However, this figure is now rapidly increasing as digital technology enables more and more people around the world to enjoy its benefits.

Francis Frith's archive is now housed in an historic timber barn in the beautiful village of Teffont in Wiltshire. Its founder would not recognize the archive office as it is today. In place of the many thousands of dusty boxes containing glass plate negatives and an all-pervading odour of photographic chemicals, there are now ranks of computer screens. He would be amazed to watch his images travelling round the world at unimaginable speeds through network and internet lines.

The archive's future is both bright and exciting. Francis Frith, with his unshakeable belief in making photographs available to the greatest number of people, would undoubtedly approve of what is being done today with his lifetime's work. His photographs, depicting our shared past, are now bringing pleasure and enlightenment to millions around the world a century and more after his death.

Southend - *An Introduction*

THE SMELL OF fish and chips, candy floss and seaweed; the sound of slot machines, motorbikes, bingo callers and fairground rides; the sight of the longest pleasure pier in the world; jostling crowds and children playing on the beach - this is the usual image of Southend-on-Sea. Yet there is more - so much more - to this popular seaside town.

The Coat of Arms tells something of the history of the town. The motto, Per Mare per Ecclesiam (By the Sea and by the Church) relates the two great influences that have affected the whole of the Southend area. As well as a monk and a medieval fisherman, there are also symbols of the four ancient parishes of Prittlewell, Leigh, Eastwood and Southchurch, each with its own fascinating history and all later incorporated into the borough.

In the Middle Ages a priory, parish church and village flourished close to the Prittle Brook. At the south end of this community, near to the sea, stood a few fishermen's huts. This was further to the east than the present centre of the town and the pier, but was the beginning of the town later to be known as Southend-on-Sea.

It was during the reign of Henry I that a Cluniac priory was first established at Prittlewell, although there had been settlement in the area long before

that, as was proved when a Saxon cemetery was discovered close by in 1923. Spears, swords and jewellery were found. It is thought that St Cedd may have built a church at Prittlewell, after re-establishing Christianity in the region in 653 AD. Artefacts from the area can be seen in the Southend-on-Sea Central Museum.

Leigh was a thriving medieval port. Many of the weatherboard cottages of Old Leigh still remain, having fortunately escaped the road development planned in the late 1940s. A fire at The Peter Boat Inn in 1892 revealed an interesting aspect of the town's past. A secret chamber was discovered, a smugglers' store from bygone days. The distinctive smell from the cockle sheds has assailed the noses of generations of visitors to the town.

Eastwood was mentioned in the Domesday Book. The entry is recorded on the wall in the parish church of St Lawrence.

Holy Trinity is the Parish Church of Southchurch. Although parts of the building are Norman, it is known that an earlier church existed here in the 9th century. Southchurch was also mentioned in the Domesday Book, with both fishing and agriculture being important at that time. The original parish boundaries included the whole of Thorpe Bay.

Stratsende or Strateshend is first recorded early in the 14th century. Meaning 'the end of the street' this is possibly the first mention of Southend. This 'street' probably ran between Prittlewell and Milton, a hamlet that was once an important port located between Leigh and Southchurch. It was not until late in the 15th century that the name 'Southende' appears to have been used. At that time Prittlewell, Southchurch and Leigh were all well established, as were Hadleigh, Rochford and many of the smaller villages mentioned in this book.

By the middle of the 18th century it became fashionable to visit the seaside. It was thought that the sea air and water gave help to those with health problems. In 1758 The Ship Inn was built and by 1768 a private company realised that the coastal area to the south of Prittlewell might be an ideal place to develop as a bathing resort. This scheme failed, but as the century wore on, an increasing number of fashionable visitors did journey from London to Southend by horse-drawn coach or by the weekly packet boat.

More accommodation was needed, and plans were made to build a grand hotel at New Southe-End, with two terraces of fine houses. The area to be developed was at the top of what is now known as Pier Hill and the name was used to distinguish it from Old Southe-End. This was the area to the east that was expanding around the Ship Hotel. By that time a few bathing huts had been introduced for the use of visitors. The new hotel was finally ready for its opening in July 1793 by which time the High Street covered the track that once ran from Prittlewell to Milton. An article in 'Gentleman's Magazine' of 1794 predicted that Southend would soon be "all

the rage".

It was the arrival of five year old Princess Charlotte and her mother Caroline, Princess of Wales, in 1801 that really made the growing town socially acceptable. The little princess was, at that time, second in line to the throne. Photographs of the well-preserved Royal Terrace, where these illustrious visitors stayed, can be seen in the following pages. Others came to enjoy the town, including Lady Hamilton (Lord Nelson's mistress), and Benjamin Disraeli. However, some people felt that Southend was too quiet!

In the early years of the 19th century the town flourished. A jetty for pleasure boats was built below the cliffs as early as 1802. Public rooms, a library and warm and cold sea water baths were opened. A steamboat service started in 1819. At this point Southend's well-known mud caused problems, as boats could not reach the shore at low tide. This led to the first wooden pier being started ten years later.

The pier was extended between 1834-35 and again in 1846, bringing its length to one and an eighth miles. This early pier was privately owned and poorly maintained. However, things improved after the Local Board bought it in 1875: re-building started and the new iron pier was opened to the public in 1889. The following year a single-track electric tramway began operating - the first pier railway in the country. Further extensions followed and by the early years of the 20th century Southend pier had become the symbol of the ever-growing town.

The pier played its part during the major wars of the 20th century. In the First World War sections came under Admiralty control and prisoners of war were taken along its length to waiting prison ships. At the commencement of the Second World War it was closed to the public and renamed HMS Leigh. It became a convoy control centre until its re-opening as a pleasure pier in 1945.

Various disasters occurred over the years. Between 1898 and 1908 the pier sustained considerable damage after being hit three times by boats. Fire too has struck with disastrous results - in 1959 the beautiful Victorian Pavilion was totally destroyed. It was replaced by a 'modern' bowling alley. Fire struck again in July 1976 when the pier head met a spectacular end. Some of the remaining charred floor supports can still be seen. In 1995 yet another fire meant the end of the bowling alley. The Pier Museum, operated by knowledgeable volunteers belonging to the Southend Pier Museum Foundation, has an excellent display of memorabilia and information on the history of this unique structure.

It was the coming of the railway in 1856 that completely changed the character of the town. Visitors no longer had to make a dangerous sea trip or endure a long and uncomfortable journey by horse-drawn carriage. They could reach the town

easily, stay for the day, and return home at night. Southend was close enough to the east end of London to make such trip a real possibility. The time of the day-tripper had arrived.

As the town flourished moves were made to gain the status of municipal borough and Queen Victoria signed the Charter of Incorporation in 1892. Great celebrations followed the reading of the Charter to a large crowd gathered at the top of Pier Hill. At this point the town was officially named Southend-on-Sea. Expansion continued and the new borough began swallowing up some of its much older neighbours. Westcliff, Chalkwell and Prittlewell had all became part of the town in 1877, and Southchurch was incorporated in 1897. Leigh-on-Sea became a part of the borough in 1913, with Eastwood and Shoebury joining in 1933. New housing estates were built for the ever-growing population. County Borough status was achieved in 1914.

Often called 'London's Playground', Southend has long been famous for its Golden Mile, Illuminations, Carnival and The Kursaal, noted for its distinctive dome. The Kursaal was opened to the public in 1901 and went on to become one of the best-known amusement centres in the country. The park finally closed in 1974. Much of the site is now used for housing, although the dome remains. The Golden Mile became a centre for amusement arcades, cafes and public houses. The annual Carnival was started in 1926 to raise money for the new Southend General Hospital and it has remained a popular event ever since.

Between the Wars the town flourished and, following the end of the Second World War, there was a brief a return to the golden age of the seaside. However, all that was about to change, due to the growing demand for a more sophisticated type of holiday.

1935 saw the opening of the Municipal Airport, built on the site of a First World War aerodrome that was used again during the Second World War. In many ways it was the growth of air travel that led to the decline of the seaside town; once it became easy to reach countries with more settled climates, towns like Southend became less attractive.

Many fine reminders of the Victorian and Edwardian ages were lost during the building boom of the 1960s and 70s. Victoria Circus was re-developed and a large shopping centre replaced Garons and The Talza Arcade. The High Street was pedestrianised and Supa-Save, built on the site of the Strand Cinema, was a pioneer of supermarket development. The beautiful bandstand, so popular with the Edwardians, was removed and a plain stage took its place. Ideas have, however, now gone full circle and a bandstand once again stands on the top of the cliffs.

The Southend area is fortunate in having some superb parks. Parts of the old Prittlewell Priory still

stand and are open to the public. In 1920 R A Jones, a prominent local jeweller and benefactor of the town, gave this delightful property to the borough. With its ancient fishponds and magnificent trees and gardens it is well worth a visit. The grounds of Chalkwell Hall became a park noted for its rose gardens. The smaller gardens around Leigh Library form a peaceful haven close to the busy centre of the town. Southchurch Hall is now a museum, but the moat and gardens take the visitor back to the time when this was an impressive manor house. The Churchill Gardens too, although small, are much loved by those working in the large civic buildings found in Victoria Avenue.

By the 1980s the old-style seaside town had declined in popularity. Trippers still came into Southend by train, coach and car, but the commercial centre of the town had moved to Victoria Avenue. Some industry developed in the area but the town needed new attractions at its 'south end'. An annual Air Show has now become popular. The Royals Shopping Centre, located at the top of Pier Hill, is well established, although the construction of this complex necessitated the demolition of many old buildings. A large aquarium is sited near the pier and Adventure Island is a must for children.

Fortunately we still have photographic records of earlier times and, within these pages, you will find some of those reminders to take you on a journey down memory lane.

For our exploration of Southend, we will approach from the west along the A13, stopping off at various towns and villages along the way. We will visit the town itself, then pause for a while in some of the towns and villages to the north, before reaching the A127 to return in the London direction.

The Approach from the West

Thundersley
The View from the Churchyard c1955 T113027
This churchyard stands at the top of Thundersley Church Road, well removed from the bustle of the town below. The church of St Peter, standing further up the hill, has a nave and aisles dating from the early 13th century. The town name is believed to have come from the pagan worship of Thunor.

Canvey Island
A Beach Scene c1955

C237065

There is little room for making sand-pies on this crowded beach. Deckchairs occupy all the available space as would-be sailors await their turn to board the motor launch 'Summer Rose'. Adults paid 2 shillings and children 1 shilling for what is described as 'a long sea trip'.

Canvey Island Thorney Bay Beach Camp c1955 C237304
Canvey Island was a popular holiday resort in the 1950s. Well-ordered rows of caravans are ready to welcome summer visitors. A complex of administrative buildings can also be seen. This photograph clearly illustrates the flatness of much of the reclaimed land that forms the island and which the sea attempted to reclaim in the devastating floods of 1953.

Canvey Island The Beach c1955 C237005
Another view of the beach at Canvey Island shows children busily playing around the many deckchairs. Most of the older holidaymakers are well wrapped up against the cold. Rather battered breakwaters give some protection from erosion to the sand and shingle beach.

Canvey Island
The Beach House Café c1955 C237122

The flat nature of the surrounding countryside is again shown in this photograph. Caravans nestle close to the large Beach House Café. This is an interesting building, with its two end towers and decorative façade. It seems too impressive for these surroundings.

Hadleigh, the High Street c1955 H167010

The Castle Hotel, with its gabled roof and solid appearance, takes its name from Hadleigh Castle. Although this photograph shows the High Street, it lacks the bustle we see today. A small garage is tucked in next to a café on the right, whilst on the left brick-built houses with fenced gardens stand alongside small shops protected by awnings.

Hadleigh, Old High Street c1960 H167014

This scene again shows The Castle Hotel, but from the west. In the intervening five years since H167010 was taken, the Esso Garage has obviously expanded, although the cottages and shops on the right are little changed. Cars have become sleeker, but note the price of the one shown on the forecourt - a snip at £226! The street lamp in this picture is less decorative than the one in the earlier view.

Hadleigh, The Castle c1955 H167008

Hubert de Burgh was granted a licence in 1230 for the construction of the castle. However, it was completely re-built in the time of Edward III. Little now remains of the massive structure that once stood on this site, although two of the towers may still be seen. A number of Plantagenet kings and their wives were associated with the castle. The building was immortalised by the artist John Constable.

Hadleigh, Central Parade c1955 H167003
This busy row of shops, with living accommodation above, faces the grounds of the ancient church of St James the Less, dating from the 12th century. Plain shop walls could be used to advertise products such as Cadbury's. The Kingsway Cinema was a popular place of entertainment in the area.

Hadleigh, The Castle 1891 29071
The castle had two main towers and a further tower guarding the entrance on the north side. There was no keep. Kentish Ragstone was brought across the River Thames for the construction. Here we see two of those towers, situated at the east end of the site. Deep cracks have appeared in the better-preserved tower.

Hadleigh, The Castle 1891 29070
This view of the towers is taken from inside the ruins. The castle stands on high ground with excellent views over the widening river. The building fell into disrepair, especially after Lord Rich bought it in 1551. Much of the stone was used in other buildings in the area.

Hadleigh, The Castle 1891 29069
Looking across the fields towards the ruins of the castle it is apparent how little remains of the original building. There are excellent walks in the area. The ruins are now cared for by English Heritage.

Leigh-on-Sea, From the West 1891 29065
Here we see Leigh at low tide with the fishing boats at anchor. Small fishermen's cottages stand behind the mounds of cockleshells, thrown out from the cockle sheds. Following outbreaks of typhoid in Southend, blamed on shellfish from Leigh, new techniques for boiling the fish were introduced at the end of the 19th century.

Leigh-on-Sea High Street c1960 L30024
This is part of Old Leigh, with the railway on the right and the sea behind the buildings on the left. The main shopping centre has moved up the hill to Leigh Broadway but this High Street is still popular with its cafes, public houses and antiques shops. There is a quaint, old-world feel to this part of the town. At one time many of these buildings were in danger of demolition to make way for a new road. Fortunately the scheme was abandoned.

◄ **Leigh-on-Sea**
The Promenade 1891

29066

Leigh is noted for its weatherboard cottages. Essex lacks natural rock so skills in the use of wood and brick-making have been well developed over the centuries. Attractive wrought iron fencing surrounds the long gardens on the right.

Leigh-on-Sea, The Cliff Shelter c1960 L30039
The Leigh sun shelter was well glazed to give protection from the wind. The glass has now gone. Fine views of the sea may be seen over the attractive flower beds. Walkers may admire the view from behind the railings on top of the shelter.

Southend, Chalkwell Park c1960 S155136
Chalkwell Park was formed from the grounds surrounding Chalkwell Hall. The Council purchased this land in 1901. It became noted for its rose gardens and as the popular centre for the annual Carnival funfair. The picture shows some of the well-kept flower beds.

Towards the Pier

Southend
Westcliff Parade 1898 41386
Many of these solid, brick-built houses are still easily recognisable today. They overlook the cliffs and the photograph is taken towards the east. Nearby, to the west, a large private house called Shorefields once stood. Now, The Cliffs Pavilion stands on this site.

Southend
Westcliff Parade 1898
41387
This view looks to the west and shows some of the same properties as in 41386, with their individual designs. A solitary horse-drawn vehicle stands in what is now a busy road. Gas lamps provided lighting at night.

▼ **Southend, Marine Gardens c1950** S155034
This photograph looks back at the same houses as those shown in 41386 and 41387. The well-laid out public gardens give a tropical air to the scene. The Lees Hotel was one of the many hotels to be found in this popular area of the town.

▼ **Southend, The Undercliff Gardens c1955** S155053
Here we see some of the gardens to the west of the main town, much enjoyed by residents and visitors. The land slopes more gently than in the Shrubbery area.

▲ **Southend The Undercliff Gardens c1955** S155056
The Cliffs Shelter, shown here, was fitted with Vita-Glass. This, it was claimed, gave the benefit of the health-giving rays of the sun to those sitting behind its protection. Walkers could stand on the roof of the shelter to enjoy the view. None of this glass remains in place.

**Southend
Westcliff Parade c1955**

S155058

This path has been built over the Cliffs Shelter, seen in the previous picture. On the left are two of the well-known hotels of the time, The Imperial and The Westward Ho! The elegant street lamps were a feature of this road.

◄ **Southend Westcliff Pool c1955**
S155047

The Southend Corporation Swimming Bath on Western Esplanade was a popular feature of the town. 300ft x 75ft, it boasted a high diving board, platforms, chutes and springboards. Dressing cubicles can be seen behind those standing on the side. Many seats were provided for spectators and there was a terrace for sunbathing.

◄ **Southend, Westcliff c1960** S155096
The West Cliff was one of the hotels in the Westcliff area and was always a popular venue for wedding receptions. Overlooking the Cliff Gardens, many of its rooms had excellent sea views. It underwent extensive renovation in the 1980s.

▼ **Southend The War Memorial c1955** S155042
The impressive War Memorial stands to the west of the bandstand on high ground overlooking the sea. Commemorating those lost in the wars of the 20th century, it is used for the annual Remembrance Day Service. The pier can be seen in the background.

◄ **Southend, Westcliff c1955** S155043
Many of the houses along this stretch of the cliff top have decorative balconies overlooking the sea. There was no problem with parking at this time, in what is now a very busy area, within walking distance of the main shopping centre. Attractive lamp posts line the pavement. In the right hand corner the fencing around the War Memorial can be seen.

▼ **Southend, The Band Stand c1950** S155032
This ornate cast-iron bandstand dates from 1909 when it replaced an earlier wooden structure. The open-air concerts held here were very popular and some shelter was provided. Note the array of chimney pots on the houses behind the shelters.

▼ **Southend, Westcliff Parade Band Stage c1955** S155059
This plain stage replaced the earlier Edwardian bandstand. Deck chairs still provided the main form of seating. The shelters remain unchanged. From the position of the flag this appears to be a windy day - possibly accounting for the small size of the audience.

▲ **Southend Westcliff Parade Band Stage c1955** S155061
Well wrapped up against the wind, holiday-makers still managed to enjoy the sunshine and music close to the band stage, using the grass verges for their deck chairs. A band can be seen performing in the background.

◀ **Southend, The Westcliff Gardens c1955** S155064
Close to the band stage and above the tree-covered cliffs are wide expanses of grass, ideal for picnics. The lady on the right looks as if she is auditioning for 'The Sound of Music', but perhaps she has been inspired by the playing of the band.

Southend, Westcliff Parade c1955 S155066

This scene looks over the top of the stage and the pier can be seen in the background. This Parade has always been a popular walking area, with its occasional views of the sea through the trees.

Southend, On the Cliffs 1898 41385

Moving closer to the main town of Southend-on-Sea, The Westward Ho! Boarding Establishment dominates this scene. It went on to become one of the premier hotels of the town. Now the name is used by a new tower block which stands on the site. A horse-drawn carriage can be seen close to the shelter, the only form of transport in sight.

Southend On the Cliffs 1891 29048

The clay cliffs at Southend have always been prone to slipping. Frequently, over the years, notices have been erected closing the threatened areas. Here we see railings lying at a very strange angle, probably as a result of this problem. The little girl, in her large hat, may have looked smart, but such clothes were certainly not designed for play.

◀ **Southend**
From the Cliffs 1895

35654

Although there are well-defined paths, the cliff gardens have yet to be laid out in a formal way. The pier and Pavilion can be seen on the right with many boats close by. A walker on the right is protected from the weather by an umbrella or sunshade.

Southend, Terraces Westcliff 1898 40913
Terraces of solid Victorian houses overlook the cliffs, with brick walls and wrought iron railings protecting the gardens. The array of chimney pots is an indication of the importance of the coal fire in those days. The cyclist is perfectly safe riding across this almost deserted road.

▼ **Southend, Royal Terrace 1891** 29061
Railings and decorative wrought iron work were both popular at this time. Royal Terrace stretches away towards the High Street. On the right are The Shrubbery Gardens. St John's Church can be seen in the distance.

▼ **Southend, Queen's Statue 1898** 41388
Queen Victoria's Diamond Jubilee was celebrated in Southend with the erection of this statue at the top of Pier Hill. Well protected by railings, the queen points regally out to sea. In later years the statue suffered from vandalism and has now been moved further to the west, near the bandstand.

▲ **Southend, The Civic Centre c1965** S155191
Moving away from the seaside, via Southend High Street, the Civic Centre is to be found in Victoria Avenue. Where once Prittlewell Church dominated the skyline now this massive Civic Centre building has taken over. Steel and glass were used in the construction of these offices, opened by the Queen Mother in 1967. The complex includes the Town Hall, Law Courts, Police Headquarters and the Technical College, all built close to the Civic Square. Victoria Avenue can be seen on the left.

Southend, Churchill Gardens c1960 S155148

This beautiful sunken garden has been created in a disused gravel pit. Following the death of the owner, the site was acquired by the town and first opened to the public in 1960. Dedicated to the memory of Sir Winston Churchill, this long, narrow garden is a delight to visit in spring when the high banks are a mass of flowers. In the background Prittlewell Church can be seen.

Prittlewell
The Village c1891
29074
Villagers can no longer stand in the middle of the street for a chat in what is now a busy road leading into Southend. Weatherboard cottages line the side of the road, close to the bridge. The little girls both wear pinafores to protect their dresses. This is a sunny day but smoke pours from a cottage chimney further along the road.

▼ **Prittlewell, The Church 1891** 29075
The Church of St Mary stands at the top of the hill above the old Cluniac Priory of Prittlewell. It dates from Norman times, but parts of an older arch, containing some Roman bricks, may be seen in the nave. The large west tower was built in the late 15th century.

▼ **Southend, The Old Priory and Park c1950** S155023
This close-up view shows the creeper-covered priory building. Some parts were destroyed and others added after the dissolution of the monasteries. The Park, noted for its beautiful trees and two large fish ponds, has always been popular with the town's residents.

▲ **Southend, The Airport c1960** S155154
Continuing north, away from the sea, we reach Southend Airport. This was used during both World Wars. By the early 1960s journeys to the Continent were becoming increasingly popular. Here we see a long queue waiting to board this Channel Airways flight, whilst many onlookers watch from the departure building.

◀ **Southend, The Priory c1960** S155145
Prittlewell Priory was a victim of the dissolution of the monasteries in 1536. Much of the building has been demolished but the refectory, seen here, remains, as does the Prior's Chamber and the cellar. At the end of the First World War Mr R A Jones purchased the house and grounds. He presented the estate to the town and it was opened to the public by the Duke of York, later King George VI, in 1920.

Southend Pier and Views to the West

Southend, An Aerial View c1955 S155044
Returning to the seaside once more this view gives an excellent idea of the way in which the town had developed by the middle years of the 20th century. The pier, with its pavilion, is clearly shown with the Palace Hotel rising above Pier Hill. The Ritz Cinema stands behind the hotel. Beyond the large open space can be seen some of the well-ordered housing development behind the sea front, typical of a town that was planned, rather than developed over many centuries. The Boating Lake and Playground dominate the foreground.

Southend, The Pier 1898 41377
Here are some of the fine Victorian buildings that graced the shore end of the pier for so many years. The iron supports of the pier can be clearly seen. Once again the walkers are well wrapped up against possible sea breezes. On the right hand side of the entrance is a weighing machine, always popular at the seaside. Out to sea, on the left of the picture, are two of the famous Thames barges with sails furled.

Southend, Pier Hill c1960 S155086
In the background of this picture stands the Gas Works jetty. Pier Hill leads down to the sea front esplanade, with the Palace Hotel on the left. Below the hotel, facing the sea, are many small shops. Towards the bottom of the hill The Gaiety Bazaar may be seen, a treasure-house for holiday gifts. Nearby the well-known Rossi ice creams are sold. A notice close to the zebra crossing advertises a Bingo Palace.

Southend, From the Pier 1898 41378

Slot machines can be seen in this picture and there is yet another weighing machine, this time on the pier itself. Wooden buttresses support the Pier Restaurant, on the hill behind Queen Victoria's statue. No one was meant to miss the advertisement for Allsop's Pale and Burton Ales above the hotel. Pier Hill rises towards The Royal Hotel and Royal Terrace.

Southend, The Pier c1955 S155068

The Pier Pavilion, once popular for concert parties and ballroom dancing, is now being used for roller skating. The Big Wheel can be seen in the playground to the right of the picture, with The Golden Hind to the left.

Southend, The Pier c1962 S155085

'Focus On America' is advertised as a free exhibition at the pier head. Such exhibitions always pulled in large crowds. Ten Pin Bowling has become a popular pastime and brought many enthusiasts to the Excel Pavilion Bowling Lanes.

Southend, The Pier from Pier Hill c1962 S155084
The old Pier Pavilion was burnt down in 1959. The Exel Bowling Lanes replaced it and live entertainment moved to the end of the pier. Steps lead up to a passenger bridge crossing over the busy Pier Hill. The small Aquarium was a popular attraction at this time, with the box office to the left selling tickets for pier entertainments.

Southend, The Beach 1898 40912
H Absalon offered bathing huts, but only for the use of ladies and children. This was where they could discreetly enter the water, hidden from prying eyes. There were other huts for men. In fact changing on the beach was officially forbidden until 1948, although, by that time, the regulation had long been ignored.

Southend from the Pier c1898 41379

This jetty was only used at high tide. The view shows more of the terraces of fine houses built above the cliffs, including Royal Terrace. It is possible here to see more of the Shrubbery Gardens.

Southend, The Beach 1898 41384
The photographer has moved in closer to the beach to take this picture, although still concentrating on the same area as the former one. The Shrubbery Gardens, above the sun shelter, are well used with plenty of wooden benches. These Victorian children are obviously enjoying their time on the beach. A number of the gentlemen are elegantly dressed with boaters to finish off their seaside apparel.

Southend
The Beach 1898 41383
In this busy scene beached boats occupy most of the shingle. However, mothers and children manage to find space and the boats form useful back-rests. The promenade is well used by walkers. Straw hats are popular for both men and women.

Southend, The Beach 1898 41381
The wooden jetty on the left would have been used at high tide. This photograph was taken long before the widening of the promenade. Most of those enjoying the sea air do so from the comfort of the long line of wooden seats below the cliffs.

◀ **Southend, The Beach 1898** 40911
Here is another view showing the popular sun shelter. With the tide in, small boats are ready to go out to sea. The Western Esplanade was not widened until 1914. Although the trees are in full leaf these Victorians, out for a stroll, are extremely well wrapped up.

▼ **Southend, The Beach c1960** S155133
Here we have a peaceful scene looking towards Westcliff. A mobile jetty is ready for use. This beach is far less crowded than those shown in the 1950s, the Indian Summer of the British seaside town. The couple in the deckchairs sit just above the high tide mark, shown by the line of seaweed.

◀ **Southend, From the Pier 1898** 41380
The Shrubbery Gardens, shown in the above picture, were first enclosed in 1825. Here, those staying in Royal Terrace or at The Royal Hotel, could walk in peace, or linger for a while on one of the benches provided. Pier Hill can be seen rising behind the foreshore buildings with the High Street stretching north from The Royal Hotel.

Southend, The Miniature Race Track 1947 S155012
The Pier Pavilion advertises 'Bubbles', a popular show at this time. Crowds have been attracted to The Miniature Race Track. For many, watching was as enjoyable as taking part in the racing. The cars, well protected with wide bumpers, speed around the circuit.

Southend, The Promenade and Amusement Park 1947 S155010
Here we see part of the amusement park again. It was known for many years as Peter Pan's Playground and lies to the west of the pier, close to the place where the previous photographs were taken. These cars were always popular. There were many other rides and attractions in the area.

▼ **Southend, The Beach from the Pier 1947** S155011
With the tide in swimmers can enjoy the water. The breakwaters were much loved by children as shingle built up on one side, leaving the other much lower. Unsuspecting visitors could be caught out, if not warned in advance about this drop. Sloping concrete blocks act as sea protection.

▼ **Southend, From the Pier 1898** 40910
Royal Terrace with the Royal Hotel on the eastern corner can clearly be seen at the top of the cliffs. Boats are drawn up on the beach close to the promenade. The foreshore buildings near to the pier include a small bandstand, suitable for open air concerts.

▲ **Southend, Pier Hill Buildings 1898** 40909
Pier Hill rises behind these foreshore buildings The clock tower surmounts the concert hall cum bandstand. This was demolished in the early 1930s. Ices, always popular at the seaside, are advertised above Zanchi's Refreshment Room on the right. Below is L Goings Beach Bazaar with some of its wares displayed on the pavement.

Southend
The Promenade c1960
S155081

This photograph was taken in the same area as 40909. Now, a wide road and Peter Pan's Playground cover what was once the beach. Many of the buildings on the right have changed little in outward appearance, although most have become busy shops protected by awnings. By 1960 more visitors were arriving by car, as can be seen from the well-parked kerb. Beyond the Aquarium are the trees of the Shrubbery Gardens.

Southend, The Pier 1947 S155009

Many of the old buildings seen at the entrance to the pier in earlier pictures had disappeared by this time. Steamer cruises had been popular for some years, with the Eagle Line taking passengers on day trips from the pier head. Pier Hill is busy with pedestrians but they seem untroubled by cars.

Southend, The Pier c1962 S155102

The lights have been hung ready for the summer illuminations. The pier was always a spectacular sight at this time of year. Well-wrapped holidaymakers manage to enjoy the sun on the ever-popular deckchairs. Ten-Pin Bowling is played in the new pavilion. Pleated skirts, of the type worn by the two young ladies at the front of the picture, were fashionable at this time.

Looking to the East

Southend
The Pier c1955 S155071
The front facade of the Palace Hotel appears on the left of the photograph with the pier stretching away out to sea. The boating lake may also be seen. The Golden Hind, its sails furled on this occasion, is beside the pier.

◄ **Southend**
The Galleon c1950

S155035

Visitors crowd the pavement and queue to board this popular and impressive attraction. The summer entertainment, 'Bubbles', is advertised on the Pier Pavilion. Those walking on the pier have a good view of the activities below.

Southend The Golden Hind and Pier c1950 S155033
The Golden Hind, a replica of Sir Francis Drake's flagship, was built 1947-48. It is on the site of an earlier water chute and swimming pool and can be seen here with sails unfurled. With the tide in, many small boats are moored close to the pier. The slope behind the boating lake was a popular place for picnics.

Southend The Golden Hind c1960 S155079
The Palace Hotel makes an impressive backdrop for this rear view of The Golden Hind. The main function rooms in the hotel overlooked the sea. The shops below the hotel can be seen and also those below Pier Hill.

Southend The Golden Hind c1950 S155038
For the sum of 6d the visitor could board The Golden Hind replica and see Louis Tussaud's Waxworks. This was always a popular attraction, especially on a windy day like this. The pier clock, seen between the masts, was a well-known landmark.

Southend, The Children's Pool c1950 S155003

This pool was to the east of the pier. Motor boats can be seen in the foreground but the pool was split in two. Canoes and rowing boats could be hired on the part closer to the pier. The Victorian Pier Pavilion can be seen in the background.

Southend, The Beach c1950 S155006
Here is another view of the boating lake, this time with the rowing boats and canoes in the foreground. The crowded Marine Parade in the background is part of The Golden Mile. This was a popular place for parents to sit in deckchairs while their children enjoyed the lake and the beach.

Southend
The Marine Lake
c1950 S155020
This view of the busy sea front, looking west across the boating lake, shows Pier Hill rising up towards the Royal Hotel and Royal Parade. The Olympia advertises 'Two Great Bands, Twice Daily'. Next door are the rounded bays over shops and beyond the imposing bulk of the Palace Hotel.

Southend, The Palace Hotel and Beach c1950 S155013
Looking east towards the pier entrance, this scene is dominated by the Palace Hotel. Once the premier hotel in the town the building served as a naval hospital in the First World War. The Olympia Arcade can also be seen with jostling crowds filling the pavement in front.

◀ **Southend, The Palace Hotel and Beach c1950** S155001

The huge Palace Hotel was built in 1904. At first named The Metropole, it served as Queen Mary's Naval Hospital during the First World War. Then, for many years, it served as a popular hotel. In recent years its role has changed, being used at one time for apartments for senior citizens and more recently to house the homeless. The boating lake was a well-used amusement in the 1950s.

▼ **Southend, Marine Parade 1898** 41382

Looking east we see fine sailing boats. These could only come into shore to pick up trippers at high tide. Awnings protect the many shops, seen in the background. This is already a busy area, well used by pedestrians.

RSAAL

Southend
The Boating Beach
c1950 S155018
At low tide holidaymakers move out onto the mud. The boats shown here will have to wait for the incoming tide to lift them level with the jetties, allowing customers to board. On the right, behind the beach, a massive gas holder can be seen. Another is almost hidden by the tree. On this site the town's gas supplies were produced. Towards the centre of the picture is the impressive dome of the Kursaal.

Southend, The Beach c1950 S155004
Sunbathers fill this crowded beach. Children now have the freedom to play in unrestricted swimming costumes, unlike their Victorian predecessors. The New Princess Maud is one of many pleasure boats seeking to take visitors for trips. In the foreground stands an unused winch.

Southend, Southchurch Hall, The Library c1950 S155028
The well-known local Dowsett family gave this beautiful moated manor house to the town. It was restored in 1930 and opened as a library in 1931. The building dates from the late 13th to early 14th centuries and was opened as a museum in 1974.

Southend, Southchurch Hall, The Lake c1950 S155026
The lake is part of the moat surrounding the timber-framed manor house, once the home of the de Southchurch family. The central hall is open to the roof beams. A Tudor extension was added to the west of the building in 1560.Here we have an excellent view of part of the moat around the brick and wooden-framed manor house. At this time the building was still used as a public library. An imposing chimney rises above the left-hand wing of the building, whilst a smaller one can be seen to the right.

◄ **Shoeburyness Ness Road c1955**

S275022

This wide junction seems to be ready for busier times to come. In the foreground stands the arch of the Conservative Club, with the solid brick-built Cambridge Hotel next door. The honey-pot style telegraph poles carry lines to the surrounding buildings.

Shoeburyness
The Promenade c1955 S275016
Shoeburyness lies to the east of Southchurch and Thorpe Bay. Small wooden beach huts line the promenade. These have always been very popular on summer days. Families often moved deck-chairs onto the pavement outside their huts. The café, advertised on the board in the foreground, stood behind the huts and was for many years known as Uncle Tom's Cabin. The beach here is mainly shingle.

Shoeburyness
The Garrison Clock Tower c1955 S275006
This imposing brick gateway, surmounted by a clock tower, was built 1860-62. A soldier stands to the right of the gate. The post box and telephone box must have been well used by residents at the camp. The Shoeburyness School of Gunnery was founded in the middle years of the 19th century

Shoeburyness
East Beach Tent Site c1960 S275095
Camping was a popular, cheap way of spending a family holiday by the sea. The tent in the foreground has a large awning, a useful way of extending the living area. This site is close to a sand and shingle beach. Roof racks were frequently used to carry extra camping equipment.

Great Wakering, High Street c1950 G100002
Wakering is noted for its low rainfall. In this picture we have a wide road and little traffic. On the left-hand side typical Essex weatherboard cottages survive, with the front door leading directly on to the street. The Lion and the White Hart public houses can be seen in close proximity on the right-hand side of the road, the latter, with its tiled roof, advertising Manns Beer.

Great Wakering, Little Wakering Road c1965 G100023
Here we see a quiet road, with rather neglected grass verges outside the houses. In the background, on the right of the picture, is the spire of the church of St Mary the Virgin, Little Wakering. The fine west tower dates from the 15th century, although the nave and chancel may be traced to Norman times.

To the North

Paglesham
The Stores c1955 P143002
Paglesham is a village of two parts, Church End and East End. In this picture the East End Post Office can be seen on the right, the one building in the row not faced with weatherboard. The small store facing the photographer also housed the Coastguard Reporting Officer. Both these buildings would have been of vital importance to the village at a time when many inhabitants had no personal transport. The buildings are still to be found close to The Plough and Sail public house, although no longer used for commercial purposes.

▼ **Canewdon, High Street c1955** C236002
There is a timeless quality about this scene and little has changed over the years, apart from the type of car in use. The Anchor stands on the corner, proudly displaying its allegiance to Manns Beers. White's Lemonade is advertised outside the shop.

▼ **Rochford, Stambridge Mill c1955** R226011
The bicycle was still a very important mode of transport when this photograph was taken. The brick-built buildings look as if they will last for another century at least. However, the huge Allied Flour Mill now stands on the site and very little of this scene remains.

▲ **Rochford, North Street c1955** R226003
Here are more Essex weatherboard cottages with tiled roofs. Notice the sign for Teas and Hovis bread over one small shop. The reassuringly solid-looking Post Office is brick built and faces the Old Ship Inn. Straight-backed cars, complete with running boards, can be seen.

Rochford, Market Square c1955 R226015
The awnings above the shops shelter busy shoppers, whilst often displaying the name of the store. An attractive street lamp can be seen in the centre of the picture. It is interesting to see the policeman stopping to chat. A market house once stood in this square, close to a water pump. Built in 1707 it was demolished in 1861.

▼ **Rochford, Market Place c1965** R226039

The town gave its name to the Rochford Hundred, an administrative area in Saxon times. This is recalled in the name of The Hundred Stationers. This square was once busy with the sounds and smells of a cattle market, but now it has been marked out for parking. Self-service super markets have become popular, this one being The Maypole. It was at nearby Rochford Hall that Anne Boleyn spent her early years.

▼ **Hockley, The Spa Hotel c1960** H176035

A spa was opened in Hockley in the early years of the 19th century and for some years was very successful, with many visitors coming to take the health-giving waters. This imposing Ind Coope hotel was built close by. The original spa building still exists in the road to the left of the picture.

▲ **Hockley, Broad Parade c1955** H176020

Continuing along the road containing the spa building, this parade of shops is to be found on the right-hand side. Hockley was a growing town by this time and a parade like this, typical of development in the 1950s, would have been well used. Shop names can be clearly seen on their shiny facia boards.

Rayleigh, The Village 1951 R224018

The village street shown in this picture is now a busy part of the town. The two cars, a motor cycle and one bicycle reflect a slower pace of life. The bank, with its solid door, is half hidden by a large tree. In the next building the International Store can be seen. This was a flourishing grocery chain at the time. The Crown Hotel proudly proclaims the sale of Manns Beer.

Rayleigh, High Street c1955 R224009
The Post Office building is solidly built of brick. Further along, on the left of the picture, the Salvation Army Chapel may be seen, with the car close by. The Co-operative Society advertisement proudly boasts that it has more than one thousand service points in London and Southend. The Southend Co-operative was founded in 1890 and later merged with the Stratford Co-operative Society.

Rayleigh, Town Centre 1957 R224027
The imposing church of Holy Trinity dominates this scene. There are some Norman traces to be found in the chancel, although much of the building dates from the 15th century. The large porch is of brick. Only the mound of the town's once important castle remains. The road is wide with unrestricted parking. Woolworth's stands beside Lipton's, another well-known grocery chain. The A127 lies to the south of the town.

Index

Southend

Around Southend

Frith Book Co Titles

www.francisfrith.co.uk

The Frith Book Company publishes over 100 new titles each year. A selection of those currently available are listed below. For latest catalogue please contact Frith Book Co.

Town Books 96 pages, approx 100 photos. County and Themed Books 128 pages, approx 150 photos (unless specified). All titles hardback laminated case and jacket except those indicated pb (paperback)

Title	ISBN	Price
Amersham, Chesham & Rickmansworth (pb)	1-85937-340-2	£9.99
Ancient Monuments & Stone Circles	1-85937-143-4	£17.99
Aylesbury (pb)	1-85937-227-9	£9.99
Bakewell	1-85937-113-2	£12.99
Barnstaple (pb)	1-85937-300-3	£9.99
Bath (pb)	1-85937419-0	£9.99
Bedford (pb)	1-85937-205-8	£9.99
Berkshire (pb)	1-85937-191-4	£9.99
Berkshire Churches	1-85937-170-1	£17.99
Blackpool (pb)	1-85937-382-8	£9.99
Bognor Regis (pb)	1-85937-431-x	£9.99
Bournemouth	1-85937-067-5	£12.99
Bradford (pb)	1-85937-204-x	£9.99
Brighton & Hove(pb)	1-85937-192-2	£8.99
Bristol (pb)	1-85937-264-3	£9.99
British Life A Century Ago (pb)	1-85937-213-9	£9.99
Buckinghamshire (pb)	1-85937-200-7	£9.99
Camberley (pb)	1-85937-222-8	£9.99
Cambridge (pb)	1-85937-422-0	£9.99
Cambridgeshire (pb)	1-85937-420-4	£9.99
Canals & Waterways (pb)	1-85937-291-0	£9.99
Canterbury Cathedral (pb)	1-85937-179-5	£9.99
Cardiff (pb)	1-85937-093-4	£9.99
Carmarthenshire	1-85937-216-3	£14.99
Chelmsford (pb)	1-85937-310-0	£9.99
Cheltenham (pb)	1-85937-095-0	£9.99
Cheshire (pb)	1-85937-271-6	£9.99
Chester	1-85937-090-x	£12.99
Chesterfield	1-85937-378-x	£9.99
Chichester (pb)	1-85937-228-7	£9.99
Colchester (pb)	1-85937-188-4	£8.99
Cornish Coast	1-85937-163-9	£14.99
Cornwall (pb)	1-85937-229-5	£9.99
Cornwall Living Memories	1-85937-248-1	£14.99
Cotswolds (pb)	1-85937-230-9	£9.99
Cotswolds Living Memories	1-85937-255-4	£14.99
County Durham	1-85937-123-x	£14.99
Croydon Living Memories	1-85937-162-0	£9.99
Cumbria	1-85937-101-9	£14.99
Dartmoor	1-85937-145-0	£14.99
Derby (pb)	1-85937-367-4	£9.99
Derbyshire (pb)	1-85937-196-5	£9.99
Devon (pb)	1-85937-297-x	£9.99
Dorset (pb)	1-85937-269-4	£9.99
Dorset Churches	1-85937-172-8	£17.99
Dorset Coast (pb)	1-85937-299-6	£9.99
Dorset Living Memories	1-85937-210-4	£14.99
Down the Severn	1-85937-118-3	£14.99
Down the Thames (pb)	1-85937-278-3	£9.99
Down the Trent	1-85937-311-9	£14.99
Dublin (pb)	1-85937-231-7	£9.99
East Anglia (pb)	1-85937-265-1	£9.99
East London	1-85937-080-2	£14.99
East Sussex	1-85937-130-2	£14.99
Eastbourne	1-85937-061-6	£12.99
Edinburgh (pb)	1-85937-193-0	£8.99
England in the 1880s	1-85937-331-3	£17.99
English Castles (pb)	1-85937-434-4	£9.99
English Country Houses	1-85937-161-2	£17.99
Essex (pb)	1-85937-270-8	£9.99
Exeter	1-85937-126-4	£12.99
Exmoor	1-85937-132-9	£14.99
Falmouth	1-85937-066-7	£12.99
Folkestone (pb)	1-85937-124-8	£9.99
Glasgow (pb)	1-85937-190-6	£9.99
Gloucestershire	1-85937-102-7	£14.99
Great Yarmouth (pb)	1-85937-426-3	£9.99
Greater Manchester (pb)	1-85937-266-x	£9.99
Guildford (pb)	1-85937-410-7	£9.99
Hampshire (pb)	1-85937-279-1	£9.99
Hampshire Churches (pb)	1-85937-207-4	£9.99
Harrogate	1-85937-423-9	£9.99
Hastings & Bexhill (pb)	1-85937-131-0	£9.99
Heart of Lancashire (pb)	1-85937-197-3	£9.99
Helston (pb)	1-85937-214-7	£9.99
Hereford (pb)	1-85937-175-2	£9.99
Herefordshire	1-85937-174-4	£14.99
Hertfordshire (pb)	1-85937-247-3	£9.99
Horsham (pb)	1-85937-432-8	£9.99
Humberside	1-85937-215-5	£14.99
Hythe, Romney Marsh & Ashford	1-85937-256-2	£9.99

Available from your local bookshop or from the publisher

Frith Book Co Titles (continued)

Title	ISBN	Price
Ipswich (pb)	1-85937-424-7	£9.99
Ireland (pb)	1-85937-181-7	£9.99
Isle of Man (pb)	1-85937-268-6	£9.99
Isles of Scilly	1-85937-136-1	£14.99
Isle of Wight (pb)	1-85937-429-8	£9.99
Isle of Wight Living Memories	1-85937-304-6	£14.99
Kent (pb)	1-85937-189-2	£9.99
Kent Living Memories	1-85937-125-6	£14.99
Lake District (pb)	1-85937-275-9	£9.99
Lancaster, Morecambe & Heysham (pb)	1-85937-233-3	£9.99
Leeds (pb)	1-85937-202-3	£9.99
Leicester	1-85937-073-x	£12.99
Leicestershire (pb)	1-85937-185-x	£9.99
Lincolnshire (pb)	1-85937-433-6	£9.99
Liverpool & Merseyside (pb)	1-85937-234-1	£9.99
London (pb)	1-85937-183-3	£9.99
Ludlow (pb)	1-85937-176-0	£9.99
Luton (pb)	1-85937-235-x	£9.99
Maidstone	1-85937-056-x	£14.99
Manchester (pb)	1-85937-198-1	£9.99
Middlesex	1-85937-158-2	£14.99
New Forest	1-85937-128-0	£14.99
Newark (pb)	1-85937-366-6	£9.99
Newport, Wales (pb)	1-85937-258-9	£9.99
Newquay (pb)	1-85937-421-2	£9.99
Norfolk (pb)	1-85937-195-7	£9.99
Norfolk Living Memories	1-85937-217-1	£14.99
Northamptonshire	1-85937-150-7	£14.99
Northumberland Tyne & Wear (pb)	1-85937-281-3	£9.99
North Devon Coast	1-85937-146-9	£14.99
North Devon Living Memories	1-85937-261-9	£14.99
North London	1-85937-206-6	£14.99
North Wales (pb)	1-85937-298-8	£9.99
North Yorkshire (pb)	1-85937-236-8	£9.99
Norwich (pb)	1-85937-194-9	£8.99
Nottingham (pb)	1-85937-324-0	£9.99
Nottinghamshire (pb)	1-85937-187-6	£9.99
Oxford (pb)	1-85937-411-5	£9.99
Oxfordshire (pb)	1-85937-430-1	£9.99
Peak District (pb)	1-85937-280-5	£9.99
Penzance	1-85937-069-1	£12.99
Peterborough (pb)	1-85937-219-8	£9.99
Piers	1-85937-237-6	£17.99
Plymouth	1-85937-119-1	£12.99
Poole & Sandbanks (pb)	1-85937-251-1	£9.99
Preston (pb)	1-85937-212-0	£9.99
Reading (pb)	1-85937-238-4	£9.99
Romford (pb)	1-85937-319-4	£9.99
Salisbury (pb)	1-85937-239-2	£9.99
Scarborough (pb)	1-85937-379-8	£9.99
St Albans (pb)	1-85937-341-0	£9.99
St Ives (pb)	1-85937415-8	£9.99
Scotland (pb)	1-85937-182-5	£9.99
Scottish Castles (pb)	1-85937-323-2	£9.99
Sevenoaks & Tunbridge	1-85937-057-8	£12.99
Sheffield, South Yorks (pb)	1-85937-267-8	£9.99
Shrewsbury (pb)	1-85937-325-9	£9.99
Shropshire (pb)	1-85937-326-7	£9.99
Somerset	1-85937-153-1	£14.99
South Devon Coast	1-85937-107-8	£14.99
South Devon Living Memories	1-85937-168-x	£14.99
South Hams	1-85937-220-1	£14.99
Southampton (pb)	1-85937-427-1	£9.99
Southport (pb)	1-85937-425-5	£9.99
Staffordshire	1-85937-047-0	£12.99
Stratford upon Avon	1-85937-098-5	£12.99
Suffolk (pb)	1-85937-221-x	£9.99
Suffolk Coast	1-85937-259-7	£14.99
Surrey (pb)	1-85937-240-6	£9.99
Sussex (pb)	1-85937-184-1	£9.99
Swansea (pb)	1-85937-167-1	£9.99
Tees Valley & Cleveland	1-85937-211-2	£14.99
Thanet (pb)	1-85937-116-7	£9.99
Tiverton (pb)	1-85937-178-7	£9.99
Torbay	1-85937-063-2	£12.99
Truro	1-85937-147-7	£12.99
Victorian and Edwardian Cornwall	1-85937-252-x	£14.99
Victorian & Edwardian Devon	1-85937-253-8	£14.99
Victorian & Edwardian Kent	1-85937-149-3	£14.99
Vic & Ed Maritime Album	1-85937-144-2	£17.99
Victorian and Edwardian Sussex	1-85937-157-4	£14.99
Victorian & Edwardian Yorkshire	1-85937-154-x	£14.99
Victorian Seaside	1-85937-159-0	£17.99
Villages of Devon (pb)	1-85937-293-7	£9.99
Villages of Kent (pb)	1-85937-294-5	£9.99
Villages of Sussex (pb)	1-85937-295-3	£9.99
Warwickshire (pb)	1-85937-203-1	£9.99
Welsh Castles (pb)	1-85937-322-4	£9.99
West Midlands (pb)	1-85937-289-9	£9.99
West Sussex	1-85937-148-5	£14.99
West Yorkshire (pb)	1-85937-201-5	£9.99
Weymouth (pb)	1-85937-209-0	£9.99
Wiltshire (pb)	1-85937-277-5	£9.99
Wiltshire Churches (pb)	1-85937-171-x	£9.99
Wiltshire Living Memories	1-85937-245-7	£14.99
Winchester (pb)	1-85937-428-x	£9.99
Windmills & Watermills	1-85937-242-2	£17.99
Worcester (pb)	1-85937-165-5	£9.99
Worcestershire	1-85937-152-3	£14.99
York (pb)	1-85937-199-x	£9.99
Yorkshire (pb)	1-85937-186-8	£9.99
Yorkshire Living Memories	1-85937-166-3	£14.99

See Frith books on the internet www.francisfrith.co.uk

FRITH PRODUCTS & SERVICES

Francis Frith would doubtless be pleased to know that the pioneering publishing venture he started in 1860 still continues today. A hundred and forty years later, The Francis Frith Collection continues in the same innovative tradition and is now one of the foremost publishers of vintage photographs in the world. Some of the current activities include:

Interior Decoration

Today Frith's photographs can be seen framed and as giant wall murals in thousands of pubs, restaurants, hotels, banks, retail stores and other public buildings throughout the country. In every case they enhance the unique local atmosphere of the places they depict and provide reminders of gentler days in an increasingly busy and frenetic world.

Product Promotions

Frith products are used by many major companies to promote the sales of their own products or to reinforce their own history and heritage. Frith promotions have been used by Hovis bread, Courage beers, Scots Porage Oats, Colman's mustard, Cadbury's foods, Mellow Birds coffee, Dunhill pipe tobacco, Guinness, and Bulmer's Cider.

Genealogy and Family History

As the interest in family history and roots grows world-wide, more and more people are turning to Frith's photographs of Great Britain for images of the towns, villages and streets where their ancestors lived; and, of course, photographs of the churches and chapels where their ancestors were christened, married and buried are an essential part of every genealogy tree and family album.

Frith Products

All Frith photographs are available Framed or just as Mounted Prints and Posters (size 23 x 16 inches). These may be ordered from the address below. From time to time other products - Address Books, Calendars, Table Mats, etc - are available.

The Internet

Already twenty thousand Frith photographs can be viewed and purchased on the internet through the Frith websites and a myriad of partner sites.

For more detailed information on Frith companies and products, look at these sites:

www.francisfrith.co.uk
www.francisfrith.com
(for North American visitors)

See the complete list of Frith Books at:
www.francisfrith.co.uk
This web site is regularly updated with the latest list of publications from the Frith Book Company. If you wish to buy books relating to another part of the country that your local bookshop does not stock, you may purchase on-line.

For further information, trade, or author enquiries please contact us at the address below:
The Francis Frith Collection, Frith's Barn, Teffont, Salisbury, Wiltshire, England SP3 5QP.
Tel: +44 (0)1722 716 376 Fax: +44 (0)1722 716 881 Email: sales@francisfrith.co.uk

See Frith books on the internet www.francisfrith.co.uk

TO RECEIVE YOUR FREE MOUNTED PRINT

Mounted Print
Overall size 14 x 11 inches

Cut out this Voucher and return it with your remittance for £1.95 to cover postage and handling, to UK addresses. For overseas addresses please include £4.00 post and handling. Choose any photograph included in this book. Your SEPIA print will be A4 in size, and mounted in a cream mount with burgundy rule line, overall size 14 x 11 inches.

Order additional Mounted Prints at HALF PRICE (only £7.49 each*)

If there are further pictures you would like to order, possibly as gifts for friends and family, purchase them at half price (no additional postage and handling required).

Have your Mounted Prints framed*

For an additional £14.95 per print you can have your chosen Mounted Print framed in an elegant polished wood and gilt moulding, overall size 16 x 13 inches (no additional postage and handling required).

*** IMPORTANT!**
These special prices are only available if ordered using the original voucher on this page (no copies permitted) and at the same time as your free Mounted Print, for delivery to the same address

Frith Collectors' Guild

From time to time we publish a magazine of news and stories about Frith photographs and further special offers of Frith products. If you would like 12 months FREE membership, please return this form.

Send completed forms to:
The Francis Frith Collection, Frith's Barn, Teffont, Salisbury, Wiltshire SP3 5QP

Voucher for FREE and Reduced Price Frith Prints

Picture no.	Page number	Qty	Mounted @ £7.49	Framed + £14.95	Total Cost
		1	**Free of charge***	£	£
			£7.49	£	£
			£7.49	£	£
			£7.49	£	£
			£7.49	£	£
			£7.49	£	£
Please allow 28 days for delivery			*** Post & handling**		**£1.95**
Book Title			**Total Order Cost**		**£**

Please do not photocopy this voucher. Only the original is valid, so please cut it out and return it to us.

I enclose a cheque / postal order for £ ....
made payable to 'The Francis Frith Collection'
OR please debit my Mastercard / Visa / Switch / Amex card
(credit cards please on all overseas orders)

Number ....

Issue No (Switch only) .... Valid from (Amex/Switch) ....

Expires .... Signature ....

Name Mr/Mrs/Ms ....

Address ....

....

....

.... Postcode ....

Daytime Tel No .... Valid to 31/12/02

The Francis Frith Collectors' Guild

Please enrol me as a member for 12 months free of charge.

Name Mr/Mrs/Ms ....

Address ....

....

....

.... Postcode ....

Free Print - see overleaf

Would you like to find out more about Francis Frith?

We have recently recruited some entertaining speakers who are happy to visit local groups, clubs and societies to give an illustrated talk documenting Frith's travels and photographs. If you are a member of such a group and are interested in hosting a presentation, we would love to hear from you.

Our speakers bring with them a small selection of our local town and county books, together with sample prints. They are happy to take orders. A small proportion of the order value is donated to the group who have hosted the presentation. The talks are therefore an excellent way of fundraising for small groups and societies.

Can you help us with information about any of the Frith photographs in this book?

We are gradually compiling an historical record for each of the photographs in the Frith archive. It is always fascinating to find out the names of the people shown in the pictures, as well as insights into the shops, buildings and other features depicted.

If you recognize anyone in the photographs in this book, or if you have information not already included in the author's caption, do let us know. We would love to hear from you, and will try to publish it in future books or articles.

Our production team

Frith books are produced by a small dedicated team at offices in the converted Grade II listed 18th-century barn at Teffont near Salisbury, illustrated above. Most have worked with the Frith Collection for many years. All have in common one quality: they have a passion for the Frith Collection. The team is constantly expanding, but currently includes:

Jason Buck, John Buck, Douglas Burns, Heather Crisp, Isobel Hall, Rob Hames, Hazel Heaton, Peter Horne, James Kinnear, Tina Leary, Hannah Marsh, Eliza Sackett, Terence Sackett, Sandra Sanger, Shelley Tolcher, Susanna Walker, Clive Wathen and Jenny Wathen.